Advance Praise

"I hope you like the powerful a1
Starts as much as I do. I especially admire how skillfully Chip Livingston makes the ordinary exotic, erotic and extraordinary."

—Ai

"The title poem of Chip Livingston's book tells us that there's "No return to the museum/Of false starts," which instantly thrusts us into the arena of paradox. But the briar patch of paradox suits this poet very well, Native American and cosmopolitan as he is, a poet who, at times, deploys the non-autobiographical invention and arresting detail of prose fiction, as well as its format and muscular rhythm. But Livingston is also easy with elaborate verseforms like the sestina, sonnet, villanelle, and triolet, which, in his hands, prove to overlap with the incantatory song tradition of Indian nations The first people on this continent recognized and deeply respected a variant human type that they referred to as "two-spirited," shamans with the power of divination and healing, artists who dressed in women's clothing and were conjugally united with other men. Livingston has updated this traditional figure to provide us with brilliant, non-routine treatments of gay experience. Not a false start at all, this first book is a distant drum announcing a fresh vision and an original approach to craft in our poetry."

—Alfred Corn

"All poets must juggle the sacred and profane and each must make some kind of peace with the paradox, fight it, or find a unique road in the up and down. Chip Livingston, in his first book, *Museum of False Starts*, makes a distinct trail of poems, through Mvskoke ancestral country, through the maze of American myths, through bars and parties at the edge, through disturbance and awe. What an auspicious beginning!"

—Joy Harjo, Mvskoke poet, musician and performer

Museum of False Starts

Poems

by Chip Livingston

Gival Press

Arlington, Virginia

Published by Gival Press, an imprint of Gival Press, LLC.
For information please write:
Gival Press, LLC, P. O. Box 3812, Arlington, VA 22203.
Website: *www.givalpress.com*

First edition ISBN: 9781928589495
Library of Congress Control Number: 2009936715
Artwork Bookcover: "Museum" Copyright © 2009 by Joyce T. Bennink.
Photo of Chip Livingston by Nicolás Arellano.
Format and design by Ken Schellenberg.

Acknowledgments

Thanks to ALL THE HELPERS, teachers, and supporters, known and unknown:

including Ai, Lee Francis, Linda Hogan, Geary Hobson, Kenward Elmslie, Suzanne Kingsbury, Cecilia Johnson, Lou Asekoff, Joy Harjo, Sherman Alexie, Charles Dearmond, Barbara Parry, Sonny Brewer, Pam White, Alfred Corn, Cyrus Cassells, Carol Poynter, Joyce Bennink, Nicolás Arellano;

to Soul Mountain Retreat, Wordcraft Circle of Native Writers and Storytellers, Native Writers' Circle of the Americas, the Arch & Bruce Brown Foundation, the Minnesota American Indian AIDS Task Force, the International Two Spirit Gathering, the Poarch Band of Creek Indians, professors and classmates at University of Colorado and Brooklyn College;

to my ancestors and the following individuals who inspired specific poems: Grandma and Grandpa Taylor, Lottie Taylor, Andrew Jackson Taylor Jr., Genevieve Veillion Taylor, Ash Jordan, my parents, sisters and brother, Wovoka, Laura and L.D. Nelson, Anna Mae Pictao Aquash, David Lynch, Hermia Alcine, Lucia Berlin, Nate Koch, Jason Reiff, Colin Cunliffe, Connor Cunliffe; and to the editors of the following journals and anthologies, where the following poems included in this manuscript were first published:

"Nelson Family Dance, 1911" in *Barrow Street*;

"Burn" in *Ploughshares* and *Best New Poets 2005*;

"Anna Mae Pictou Aquash, 1976," "*Loxosceles reclusa*," "Let's do this again" and "Straight Acting" in *Cimarron Review*;

"Coon Wash Here, 1985" and "With Fire" in *McSweeney's Internet Tendencies*;

"Apalachee Tuscaloosa" in *Brooklyn Review*;

"Woodcut" and "Horsewalker" in *Mississippi Review*;

"Luzca Bien" in *Square One*;

"Absence is not here" in *New American Writing*;

"Shake Rattles" in *Harrisburg Review*;

"Ghost Dance" in *Boulder Planet*;

"Arachnophobia" and "Arachnophilia" in *Rosebud*;

"Defuniak Springs" in *Gargoyle*;

"Nocturnal Admission" in *Velvet Heat*;

"Confessions of Brotherhood," "The True Gentleman Joins a Fraternity" and "Lion Watch" in *ALARUM*;;

"Creation Myth" and "*Pica pica*" in *Backwards City Review*;

"Praisin' Jesus" in *Lodestar Quarterly*;

"The Favorable Witness" in *MiPOesias*;

"Standing Still" in *Argestes*;

"Yesterday My Father was Dying" in *Stories from the Blue Moon Café Vol. 3*;

"The Best Way to Eat a Mango" in *In the Family*;

"Sunday, Francis Bay" in *Hampden-Sydney Poetry Review*;

"Boca al Lupo" in *Rhino*;

"Full of Aloha" and "Quiscalus quiscula" in *Yellow Medicine Review*;

"Summer Marriage" in *Apalachee Review*;

"The Museum of False Starts" in *Smartish Pace*.

for Ash Jordan and A.J. Taylor Jr.

Table of Contents

II.

III.

I.

Nelson Family Dance, 1911

Two bodies swinging like a portrait of breathing
Shadows on the North Canadian River
Live oak leaves rasping over gravel
And bird song impossibly still
Scoring the hush of reason
A moment spent imagining our future

Their heads turned as if hedging against futures
The Nelsons danced in silhouettes stopped breathing
Laura's arms loose by her sides like twice as many reasons
Her skirt torn thistledown light — she was river
Walking, free of gravity that anchored me to gravel
And my private rite of standing still

Hung between black water and the bridge's steel
Half-inch hemp rope noosed a woman from her future
Vigilante justice struck without a gavel
Okemah's court all there to see this thing
Night terror witnessed by the river
Where I memorized the swollen face of Laura Nelson

And 20 feet away — 14 and yellow — her son
L.D. swayed to face his mother and a mob no longer hostile
I prayed for them beside the river
Betting deeds to lay as tokens on our future
And begged to never witness anything
Again so grave

As a boy cattle-stringed above the grave
Hands behind his back — kept from reaching for his mother
or for reason
My conscience could not settle this, my first lesson in
lynching
But I joined the crowd and climbed the mount of steel
Posing for the photo bridging judgment to the future
Sealing purgatory there above the river

If history is as long as this river
And my vision isn't buried in my grave
Let the untried present fair-effect the future
And speak to a territory's daughters and sons
I was smiling as the Nelson family's dancing stilled
I was standing on the bridge, I was breathing

Be a secret thing beside the river
Under gravel, hanging still
Above the brittle steel of reason's future

Burn

That owl was an omen
Driving home from the airport
Not once but twice
It rose in my headlights
From rain black asphalt
Great white wings nearly touching
Windshield wipers   that low flying escort
Stretching sixty miles toward Alabama
The owl was always right
Something died and something else
Was just about to
I checked my daughter's red-eye slumber
In the rearview mirror
No need to worry her with divination
An hour drive delayed by rain
And now this trepidation on the slick black road
Certain as miscarried fortune
Her coming home to Mama in an autumn storm
And no such thing as California
Just a red clay creekbed down the road
From the house I birthed her in
Filling up to bathe away a sorrow
Blinking lights behind us
Before I hear the sirens
Firetruck passes on the narrow bridge
Then Crabtree Church in flames beyond the graveyard
My daughter wakes and guesses lightning

But I never heard the thunder crack
And only saw the lightning white of dreaded wings
I pull in   step out   open an umbrella
Stand with the firemen   watch the frame fall down
The Marshall asks if we saw anything
Like kids driving away in a four-wheeler
They found tracks in the mud
Whiskey and beer bottles   a gas can
Burn! All those years of homecoming
Annual dinners on the grounds
Hymns around a weather-warped piano
Burn! My granddad's Indian education
Walls that heard a thousand lessons
A thousand prayers in high soprano
Burn! Fifty paper funeral parlor fans
Cokesbury hymnals and sixteen pews
Reduced to flakey carbon tamped with rain
The death of wood and glass
And half a baby's ashes in my daughter's pocketbook
All the little names we'll never sing
I aim to find that messenger again and scare him off
Litter the road with his insolent feathers

Anna Mae Pictou Aquash, 1976

I speak my story in Micmac
tongue from beyond
You hear me in English
Lakota, Cree
in the misting rain
or torrents still
not strong enough
to wash my blood
from your hands

The hands tell the story
all the gory details
how I followed the sun
and traveled west
left my children
and hands in the snow

Right up to the point
I was exhumed
they called me Jane Doe
A proper Lakota burial
it was raining
gave me back my name
Anna Mae

Where are my hands?
Still in Washington?
Destroyed or sold
to some collector?

I want them back
The turquoise slides from
my wrists
I can't
pick up my children
collect the rice
play the guitar

I want them back
I want it all back

Coon Was Here, 1985

I never called you Coon
though that was home Ricky
brother I still think is God
& pray to   bound by half our blood.
Mom's firstborn   by a non-Indian
you came out blond & blue-eyed.

I got my Daddy's Choctaw eyes.
And eyes are what made Poocha call you Coon.
Crazy bastard   with all your Indian
names.   On your headstone it says Ricky.
But wolf is what you carried in your blood.
Poocha took it straight from God.

And whose eyes are bluer than God's?
Yet you put Mom's mascara to your eyes.
& burning them you tried to brown your blood.
Fisting them tattooed you like a ring-tailed coon.
From then on Poocha never called you Ricky.
But named you Coon, 'cause you were Indian.

Then named you again in secret   in Indian
& told you how your grandma bet the wolf his eyes
& won.   I miss you so much Ricky,
I swear to God.
I thought you were smarter than a damn raccoon,
letting a bunch of rednecks make you doubt your blood.

By 17 you'd made spilling blood
a ceremony & finally learned to kick ass like an Indian.
You even hung a coon-
tail from your Pinto's rearview mirror.   Eyes
still red from dope & daring God
behind your bangs.   Then you did it Ricky.

You made the papers as a Richard.
But I want to write your name in blood
on the wall behind Geronimo's Spirits   where God
took you to rest with the Indians
through a western door where no one sees your eyes
& no one calls you Coon.

I'll write *Coon was here* & sign it Ricky
call you God & mix your blood
to paint forever closed your Indian eyes.

Apalachee Tuscaloosa

Get off that white horse, elder
Take off that headdress
Throw it in the red brain
of earth   clay
No horse culture
No TV plains or pintos
though horseback postcards
at the reservation gift shop
go fast as dreamcatchers
and sweet potato pralines
You're a pecan pickin fisherman
Pray to that bait bumpin stumpknocker
Pray to that deer
in your bow knuckle
Pray to that sugared pecan
rotting in your Aunt Lottie's foot
Throw those Technicolor feathers
into the green sky
Let them fly in red clouds
like suns coming out
from under water
Pray to the hair you shake out
Pray to the onion you hoe

Woodcut

I watched death's angel lead a little sister and her brother out their bedroom window. They don't remember leaving the house. Death was a woodcut thick as deep night. I watched them sleep beside the river, watched them curl into the wet sawgrass. I didn't see death's sparked step home, where their parents slept above a faulty circuit breaker. I heard the gas roar and saw the moon in flames. It woke up little sister—left us orphans.

Horsewalker

Horsewalker sounded like an Indian name, but my grandfather denied it. Trouble came to men, he knew, of every skin and age, and at eleven, he was unable to hide it. The commander sent him home to grow another year, but grandpa ran away and joined again. He'd been a man at ten, and finally found the men who needed him, in a western Mississippi regiment more lenient than the prior one had been, a corps that counted Rebel dead before he'd come and changed their war. They swore him on as drummer boy, but he became their drum—the lucky totem day and night they beat upon.

Loxosceles reclusa

As father thumped
my 14-year-old kneecap,
swollen watermelon size,
to see if it was ripe,

he reminded me
tough boys don't cry,
but my flesh wailed
from the "pimple"
the "ingrown hair"
the "boil"
popped between
two angry thumbnails
chewed past their quicks.

Not a boil.
Not a pimple.
But flesh red and black
and rotting from a Brown Recluse
pulled crumbled from my football pants,
pads donned to prove a quiet son's worth.

The spider bite was diagnosed
by a white doctor at Indian Health,
dad having dropped me off
reluctantly on his way to work.

The poison ate away
at the saved leg,
elevated seven days,
the growing hole salved
with two tubes of antidote an hour
and melted with clear plastic Saran wrap
inside a borrowed heating pad
into my throbbing leg.

Today a dime-sized scar
indents a kneecap
tender when it rains.
And thirty years of spider medicine
weave me back to Alabama
and my father,

now his limbs arthritic;
hair gray;
skin gray;
eyes arachnoid
– cataractous.

Luzca Bien

shine well you lover of dandelions   blue bells
deaf cats and conversations with finicky stowaways

suitcasing a stolen holiday to   that light   to
chance   your girlish skip in the shadows of flatirons

a bandit to two-step   to shine   like the Calais
summer morning lifts   a pond   lifts

Veronica Lake from a fog/sheen/mist   the last
letters   unprinted   unsent   but clear

as the passion of skunks   those two
whose love would draw you to witness

amorous eclipses underneath a yellow moon
you wrote of lunar cycles growing full

recognized all animal minstrels   the web-footed
annuals   connecting gardens by streams

and every pollinator in between   the daffodils
the dirt daubers on the water iris   the lizards

in the sage   light crannied into cracked china cups
polished by a lapis hand   like a Carib's

green eyes above a blue quartz wave   your latest
heavenly coup unmissed   the wisp of a ghost dog's

wet nose meshed against a white screen door
like a secret you want to yell   so you whisper

Absence is not here

Last from every forest
Here we're without anonymity

Your nameless ends without end
You are not the last to be silenced

You knew not where to fall   that two
Or three less boys might just be the end of the world

And surely we haven't forgotten   the many reptilian
Beasts pulled from your hips   "Absence is not here" you
whispered

We learned nothing out of ignorance   no forgotten
cameras
Nothing   inside no furnace

Clear insectless morning
You wonder what else

Earlier this silence   while everything stopped
Absence is not false   death can't be nothing

An unknown place   maybe is us
Your sockless foot against timelessness

This stops loosely   loosely from yours
Not like absence doesn't intend to leave

Shake Rattles (a stomp dance)

Rattles shake   I dance   Leader calls   I mimic
Ape words   I don't understand   No drum   Beat
changing   Then consistent   Rhythmic   And mother,
sisters, aunts, grandmothers stomp   Turtle shells
Tied around their legs   Shakers rattle   I too
Wantthemtiedaroundmine Notmytradition Genderforbids
Twospirits   Once recognized   Man Woman   We-wah
Don't argue   Not my place   I dance silent   Stomp red dust
Backwards around the fire   Backwards I dance coyote
I dance crow   I dance rabbit Trickster, I dance   I am   Lost
No bustle   Not my tradition   Black hat   White
feather   Sister silent smiles   Our tradition   I smile
dance with me   Take my hand   Dance backwards
Forward   Faster   Circle in a square   Sacred   I
smile   I dance   Sister smile   Mother
smile   Father smile   All my relations
smile   Dance   Stomp   Shake rattles

Ghost Dance

I think I'm going crazy when I see my reflection
in the camera's lens. I'm surrounded by the dead. Jimi,
Marilyn, Joan — face covered in cold cream, hand holding
wire hanger high above her head. The Halloween Parade
has paused for television crews in front of The Revolver on
Duvall Street in New Orleans. I duck inside for a drink,
take the elevator to the thirteenth floor.

I walk inside the club without ID. Tonight I don't
need it. Tonight I'm invisible. I pass witches, goblins,
boys dressed like ghouls. Once we were two of them.
Once we both joined the annual masquerade. But tonight
is different. Tonight I don a plain white sheet with
ink. Circles traced around holes cut out to see through.
Another hole through which I drink, from which I breathe.

I wasn't coming out tonight. Didn't plan or
purchase a costume. Wouldn't wear one hanging in your
closet. What led me to the linens then, to quickly cut a
cotton sheet into a kid's uniform? What drove me to this?

Beneath this sheet, your medicine bag hangs around
my neck, the tanned leather pouch you made me promise
never to open. This is the first time I've worn it. But no
one can see it. No one can see me.

I finish my drink, scotch neat, with a gulp, sing the
invisible song you taught me, set the glass on the black
wood rail, and, still singing, step onto the dance floor.

Beneath this sheet, I imitate you dancing. My
feet, awkward at first, soon find your rhythm, and my

legs bounce powwow style in the steps we both learned as kids. The steps that never left you. I dip and turn between, around the fancy dancers in their sequin shawls and feather boas. I shake my head like you did when your hair was long, the way you flipped it, black and shining, to the heavy beat of house music. The music hasn't changed much in case you're wondering. I dance in your footsteps; sing the invisible song; close my eyes.

When I open my eyes, I swear I see Carlo. Impossible right, but he's stuffed inside that Nancy Reagan red dress and he's waving at me, sipping his cocktail and smiling. He's talking to Randy, who's sticking out his tongue that way he always did whenever he caught someone staring at him. I start to walk over but I bump in to Joan.

She's glaring at me. Or it may just be the eyebrows, slanted back with pencil to make it look like she's glaring at me. She reaches past me and grabs Marilyn by her skinny wrist and pulls her away, but Carlo and Randy are gone. Where they stood are faces I don't recognize. Faces dancing. Masks I realize. Faces behind masks.

The DJ bobs furiously with pursed lips, headphones disguised as fiendish, furry paws, in the booth above the floor. He introduces a new melody into the same harping beat, and I remember to dance. I remember you dancing. My fingers sliding across your sweaty chest, I find the necklace. The sheet clings to my body in places. The new song sounds just like the last song but I'm being crowded together with strangers. I can no longer lift my legs as high as I want to, so I sway in place, shuffle with the mortals on the floor.

Behind me someone grabs me, accidentally perhaps, but I turn violently, jealously. There are too many people in this equation. Two become one again and again, and ones become twos. All around me real numbers add up to future possibilities. Imaginary numbers. It's why we're here dancing.

A cowboy nods his hat in my direction. But he can't be nodding at us. We're invisible. I think maybe he is a real ghost; he's peering intently into the holes cut out for my eyes. He looks like Randolph Scott, blond and dusty, so I look around for Cary Grant as Jimi lifts the guitar from his lips and wails. Randolph Scott is coming this way and I turn my back and dance.

I want you back, Elan. I want you back dancing beside me. I start chanting this over and over to myself. I want you back. I want you back.

You taught me the power of words. I believed you. I can even smell you now. Sandalwood oil and sweat. I turn and expect to see you.

Not you behind me.

Not you beside me.

Not you in front of me.

Not you anywhere around me.

I make my way to the bar, but the bar is too crowded. The barman's face grimaces over hands holding folded dollars as he tries to keep the glasses filled. The air is thick with bitter smoke. It's hard to breathe. I make my way for the door, notice the cowboy trailing me. In the elevator, I go down alone.

Into the rain on Duvall Street, we walk out together. One set of footprints splashes our muddy way toward home, then, turning, I realize we are not going home, but passing more pagan tricksters decked out as holiday spirits.

The bells in the clock tower tell me it is midnight. Squeaking from its hinges, the door to morning slowly opens and it's All Saints Day, the Day of the Dead, and I am walking toward Boot Hill, to where you are buried.

We're alone in the cemetery. And the wind lifts the rain in a mist rising up from the wet earth which is claiming me. I remove my sheet in front of the cement memorial that holds your body up above the boggy ground. I remove my shoes. I strip off everything except your leather pouch around my neck, and I dance for you. My legs are free and I whirl and sing.

I'm dancing for you now, because you loved to dance. I want you back dancing. I want you dancing now.
I'm dancing for you now, because you loved to dance. I want you back dancing. I want you dancing now.
I'm dancing for you now, because you loved to dance. I want you back dancing. I want you dancing now.
I'm dancing for you now, because you loved to dance. I want you back dancing. I want you dancing now.

II.

Arachnophobia

That spiders fall like stars on strings from trees and ceilings of garages scares the shit out of my tough little sister, a chemist with a PhD who got a pistol from her husband for her twenty-sixth birthday. My little sister, who played in darts tournaments with mustached gay cowboys at the Round Up on Thursdays, and "whipped their asses," who used to hunt deer with our father and race motorcycles with her boyfriends. She sees spiders now when she closes her eyes. She doesn't sleep at night. She stays inside and dusts the closets. She won't sit down until she pounds the cushions on the couch. She shakes out her throw blanket and pulls her legs beneath her lap – the way a spider folds its legs when it's about to pounce. My little sister is ready to jump out of her skin. My little sister thinks spiders sense her fear and are drawn to it, spiders who thought her up. So she won't garden; her cats have allergies; she has six exterminators on rotation. My little sister is afraid one exterminator will find out about another, at a convention or an expo. Her husband doesn't even know because she uses her own money. But his head aches behind his eyes when he gets home. He thinks it's her.

Defuniak Springs

Ready with the minute hand,
walking the shore of isn't asked,
among cypress mud, little knees shrugging
their watch, the crappie bedded
in pebbled water, us mumbled
by their congregation, by
what swayed forth, assumptions
mussing the whispered shoulder,
the fist-sized thought, head testing
the crisis reached — we stumbled
into symptoms, shadows
turning water into turning water,
the stumpknockers' spasms liquid
against root, against autumn,
and just before we turned into roads,
your eyes were wide as a cottonmouth's strike
feeling the quake of a step,
and nature completed the truth of the matter,
stomached a subject unalterable:
We were four-footed, with appropriate clouds,
and how much like gravestones
were your slate buttons.

Nocturnal Admission

I went to my mother's room at 13
past midnight, and told her I was dying.
I'd wet the bed, I'd had this crazy dream,
about a sexy neighbor I'd been spying
on. Well, I didn't tell her that, I mean,
the day before she asked who I was eyeing
when I didn't want to go outside
for ice cream. The truck was parked out front,
and she was buying, but I couldn't join
the other screaming kids —
not with Lance applying suntan lotion
to his muscled teenage skin.
Stretched out on a beach towel
in his front yard, his body mystified me,
while mine seemed happy to defy me.
My dick would tent my cut-offs
at the sight of him.
I wore two pair of underwear,
but even then I thought I'd burst
right through the seams.
So I didn't dare tell mother what I'd dreamed,
though she did think to ask me.
I'd have been a fool to tell her that.
She thought my blush was any boy's,
puzzling out his sexuality, but I swear it was
as much because the fantasies
were always other boys,

some from my baseball team,
some the roughnecks at school,
but usually Lance. He was flying
naked in the dream I had that night,
the one that made me think that God
was mad and killing me. I was lying
(also naked – and hard as cinder block)
on the beach towel I'd seen him lay
across the grass the day before.
I tried to understand the signs implying
I might turn into some kind of freaky thing.
But it would have been cruel to tell my mother that,
especially when she was already crying,
and trying not to laugh at the same time,
when I showed her what came out of me.
She apologized for throwing such a scene,
said I was growing up to be a man, that's all it meant,
said it was normal for a boy my age's thing
to start uprising like a metal beam.
She apologized again
that I didn't have my dad around to train
an 11-year-old boy in the ways of puberty.
I was as stupefied as I've ever been.
She never mentioned him.
And I have never turned a deeper red
than I did then, at 26 past midnight,
when my mother helped me change my sheets,
and said the next day she'd teach me to wash them.
And then she said she'd ask the man across the street

to talk to me. Would that be okay?
Or would I feel more comfortable
with someone younger, like his son?

Straight Acting

My waking up in Whitney's car would take
some puzzling through — fist fight at Pizza Hut?
The parking lot, Whit said to fake me out.
To fake my father really, knowing I was drunk,
too drunk to tell a lie. "A fight with who?"
I asked. The youngest Boatright boy. "And why?"
Whit didn't know why Ben had bloodied me.
He didn't know if he should take me home
or to the hospital for stitches.
I said, "Call my dad," who came to pick me up,
ignoring beach sand falling from my jeans,
my vomiting in Whitney's kitchen sink,
my running into him on the way out Whit's front door
and falling down. In the car Dad asked me
what I'd had to drink, and where.
I said, "Southern Comfort and grape Icey."
He laughed, "Pizza Hut, huh?"
I shrieked at home when he cleaned my eye
with alcohol, and taped the cuts,
then popped a beer can open before breakfast.
His wife said I deserved to be sick
ruining good liquor like I had, but Dad
just drank his beer and looked a little wise
and sideways as he smiled at me.
I felt better by afternoon
when Audrey's call had clarified the why and where.
The Boatright boy had been her date

and she and I'd been sitting on Ben's Dodge
at Pensacola Beach, a party Dad forbade me to attend
at just fourteen. Drunk, I'd wobbled from my memory,
and Audrey grabbed my face as I passed out.
Ben saw her hand extend to take my chin.
And assuming that a kiss was coming next, he rushed
and hit me after I lost consciousness.
My blood on the white hood was the talk
of school on Monday, graduating me, unknown freshman,
to upperclassman fame: as a drinker and a ladies man,
they thought they knew my name.

Confessions of Brotherhood

I fed my little sister to the lion
to prove I was as man as other men
reveling in bourboned rebellion
I fed my little sister to the lion
offered her a Greek cotillion
watched her idol worship end
I fed my little sister to the lion
to prove I was as man as other men

The True Gentleman Joins a Fraternity

1. RUSH WEEK

delicate guest in the air-chanted season
questioning questioning geometry
the first limitation reforming men
that good must last genius in practical conduct
more geometry dictation
men pound practical geometry
huge—the first limitations

2. THE TRUE GENTLEMAN

some nature compels joy, backwoodsmen
fantastical giants to man nimbly other
his nature compels mysteries namely
intention over astronomy
solution—divinity

3. LINE-UP (A DINNER MENAGERIE)

a man—magically Neapolitan
he forms talents devouring fate
something first ulterior
far 'jaculating candle
independent counting-rooms
where any body could cosset perception

4. HAIL TO THE PURPLE

devotion with exasperations
sometimes conspicuous gauntlet
—politics, refinement
seems lean bold manly by form
burgesses quite vascular
swindler in a precisely
—right arterial instinct
luxury ice midsummer
moment familiar
grinding softest sentinels

5. THE PHOENIX

conduct cringes sympathy
[skipping] his poverty
[skipping] achievements
company, crisis other feelings
emergencies his gentleman word
[skipping] patterns
[skipping] feeling

6. HAIL TO THE GOLD

less long engendered tyrant
the coarse state like handicrafts
their legislatures the neighborhood
explosive destined lion
soldiers stream the ceasing legs
supreme ladders—himself after dream

excellencies, governors
course to community harmony
his must America

7. HELL WEEK

well, it decomposes mind matter
justice, man, for elements escape contradiction
flippant mistaking facts command
mistaking salute to think talk held conduct
atmosphere, mind atmosphere—only justice, man

8. IN THE BONDS

man's key is like any
majority habit: life
maintenance intrepid performance mark
labors like manures, waters
poured deeper, more namely
boy into man day
fibre becomes man
interests with consequences
desperate easily days
war, race—any bible inventory
man's faculties, mind goes
makes nature public
necessary majorities

Lion Watch

In keeping with their brotherhood,
their brotherhood was kept, round the lion
Where the nineteen of them stood.
In keeping with their brotherhood,
a brother knew a brother would
be one he could rely on.
In keeping with their brotherhood,
their brotherhood was kept around the lion.

To My Family Members Who Read

Dear Mom and Dad:

    I'll start with you, and ask you not to take offense at what I had the parents do in that last published story. It fit, that's all, and everyone assumes it's fiction. Even if they did have your names and some of your characteristics. You're what I know; I added in the child abuse for conflict. It drove the plot, and is not an insight into how I think you raised me.

Mom:

    You want me to take those "fucks" back. But those "fucks" are for emphasis. They sting your ears, so I wouldn't use the word for all the world if I knew a better one. You should also know that if I use the word "fuck" — even if I use it to mean *fuck* — it doesn't mean I'll use the word "fuck" in front of you.

Dad:

    You get the brunt of all my young, male protagonists' rage. You see yourself in every dead and absent father. You don't like seeing yourself that way. But my characters are at the age where everything their parents do annoys them. I went through that. We had a fight or two. I just make up stories.

Lucky Sisters:

Four of you—each married, kidded. I admit I
like to watch you point your fingers, hear you say things
like, "That's Christie, isn't it?" when you know full well
who had the boob job. The young, married women in my
stories are not you. I don't care how you raise your kids.
If you feed them ice cream before bed and then complain
when they don't sleep, who am I to think that there might
be a better way? I don't have children of my own.

Brother:

I have never written down about the time you almost
drowned when you were three, how blue you were and
dead, resuscitated and Life-Flighted to hospital. Comatose
days. Snapped to and asked Mom for something to drink.
I've relived that week, imagining your heaven. You don't
remember anything. But I know why nothing ever bothers
you, and why you cry at Hallmark commercials. You *know*
there's nothing to worry about. I won't write a word about
you. I promise.

And with closets full of cousins, imagine all the stories
on the hangers. But dear, sweet members of my family,
I urge you not to see yourselves in my fictitious mothers
and sisters, my fathers and brothers, even my wicked
stepmothers.

Except for my mom's brother Dick and his third wife Kat (his former secretary, pregnant when they married):

You may see yourselves in every hateful-minded hypocritical Southern Baptist I've ever written about. They were based absolutely on and directly from watching the two of you.

Creation Myth

Crawfish's idea   digging the mud up
But who thought up Columbus

Mud a man can sail to   flown through fog
And down down into mountains

My own breath part of that naming
Esakitaumessee   Fuswalgi   Chebon

Until we got the hang of marrying down   down   down

Not the very best idea   remember Atlantis
All that water   first deal with birth mother

Never in SF at the same time   in case it happens again
Never play piano under water   listen to piano music
under water never

There are legendary comparisons how could it be
The Christian reincarnate of a drowned woman

Listen   if you think it's noisy in my head

Praisin' Jesus

National Day of Prayer Ceremony, Emancipation Garden,
St. Thomas, V.I.

Because the cancer was in only one breast,
and even though the man won't come back
the hair will,
meanwhile wigs are nothing new
to me, praise Jesus.

I got away from Daddy.
And, praise Jesus,
my cancer got my 6-year-old
away from hers.
Jesus, you're the only man
who broke the cycle
of a father's rage.

My hands are high
and my closed eyes
show glory and forgiveness;
Thanksgiving hymns
spring from my lips,
oh Father,
but just between you and me,
I'm not convinced
you're any different.

So just in case, Lord,
I'm praisin' sweet Jesus
for the chance to wear pants,
my hair short,
and the new ways
you've shown me
to love another woman.

The Favorable Witness

Truckstop refinement is hell,
little turning club for public sailors
confessing voyeur mates' fates;
spying, I mean, outside my *No such
house* and its slatted admission.
Remembering where strangers stood,
Hercules' determination, me buried,
the mist sheet of anonymity.
Remembering screams' tight smiles,
the homesick circuit, miracle falls
of release; facts consequences desperate
for sleep, mood bottles, mount posing,
rushed white while sisterman watched.
Not father alone. Remember,
father's me. Remember earned embrace.
We were animals there, mouths watering,
men watching cut awkward, being
themselves before being belonged.
Remember the year through fever,
the returned, the recovered. Remember
yesterday's map of my father. Ratified
indulgence, fervor, devotion. Had I

one illuminato fearless? Had I one
favorable witness? Had I the illusion
of meeting the one actually allured?

Standing Still

1.

I am standing still looking at the ground. The preacher reads holy words that mean nothing. There is no comfort spoken from the book that colonizes, oppresses, doesn't recognize you or me. They lower you into the ground and mother throws in your turtle rattle. She is holding on so tightly, she nearly forgets to let go.

2.

She nearly forgets to let go and swings out farther than she means to. The shallow water reflects the same sun as the deeper, safer depths. Swinging shadows move as she falls, kicking legs wildly in a wheeling arc. Splashes with a crack, down then up again, exploding from the river where Pucv and all my relations bathed before we were civilized.

3.

We were civilized in our fancy dress hotel. We were civilized with our martinis and white drugs. We were civilized as we signed the bar check with a number and went back to order room service.

4.

Room service includes towels, trays, and trysts when you're snowed-in in Aspen during international gay ski week. It's the Pretty People Party and you're stuck there, with no way to get out, so you do what the pretty people do. You walk the halls, the dining rooms, the floors in

your suite. You're too wired to stand still. You search the
other guests like a vulture, looking for a body to occupy,
to release your energy. The pent-up energy of all these
gym clones is suffocating. The circling the stalking the
desperation of Tom.

5.
Tom bumps into me in an empty banquet room. What
am I doing here he wants to know. Looking for the bar.
Looking for you if you want to know the truth. Looking
for fountains of Wayne. I need to walk this off, I say. The
snow is intense. Tom invites me up to his room for a drink,
to smoke some grass, to relax, maybe a massage. I'm too
fucked to fuck, I say, even if you are a natural beauty.

6.
Natural beauty doesn't do it anymore. It takes
development, condos, theme parks, playgrounds. It takes
power. It takes a handful of drugs and a scotch to wash
it down. It takes a bump to get it up and, since coming
isn't possible, a joint to get back to earth. I think I hear
someone at the door. I hide in the bathroom, the door
locked, shaking. I rinse my face with cold water. I try to
blow my nose, waste all this good coke, but I can't breathe.
9,000 feet. Maybe it's the altitude.

7.
"Maybe it's the altitude," Tom says, but I think he says
Maybe it's the attitude. "Maybe it is," I reply, But
everyone has it, the attitude sickness. Sick of granite gym

tits, sick of E queens dancing with their dicks shrunk into
their nuts, sick of Grievous Bodily Harm to get a rock off.
Sick of Madonna's *Don't Cry For Me* remake.

8.
Remake the land, remake the language. Make a new
beginning with the beauty and the love and the goddess.
Let us go into the light and start over. Medicine pouch
around my neck and pockets full of crystals. Smoke the
sacred pipe and send prayers to Mitakuye Oyasin—All
My Relations. Buddhist chanting Hail Mary's inside
a pentacle—astral traveling to Mecca. To Nirvana. To
Galt's Gulch. To Aspen.

9.
Aspen is the pinnacle of success for leather queens in
furs. Fur is dead. Save the unborn transgendered Native
American whales. Recycle, reuse, resurrect the dead.
Here, let me hold your head. A bump of crystal will pick
you up. You'll feel great. Are you throwing up? Maybe it's
the altitude. You've got to develop a stomach for this. We
might be stuck here till Thursday or Friday. I've got to get
out of here, I say. You can't go anywhere. Nobody can go
anywhere. Maybe you should get some rest. Do you want
something? Let me see what I have.

10.
I have about 45 minutes until you're covered with dirt,
filled over with earth. Back to where we came from. You
go where we're all going. I have 45 minutes left to join you.

Jump in and Please God, Please alltheloveintheworld,
Please take me with you.

11.
With you beside me below me on top of me I could do
anything. Do not leave me. Tears mix with rain and make
a muddy grave. I hear you speaking through thunder.
What's that? But I can't wait. I can't hear you. The wind
blows the chain against the flagpole. We forgot to take
the I-pledge-allegiance-United States-flag down when it
started raining.

12.
When it started, raining clouds covered the sun and the
shadows stopped moving. I never looked up to see what
moved between the sun and the grave, between the sky and
where you were being lowered into the ground. I imagined
it was eagles, wheeling above lending strength, carrying
you to the spirit world in feathered arms.

13.
Feathered arms marked by mourning, black bands
wrapped tight around crow feathers. One-hundred crying
wounds from mother's attempt to go with you. Wailing
piercing screams of sorrow. Aunts, uncles, grandfathers
rush to her side as the last shovels of wet earth cover you.
The sun comes back suddenly warm. All your pagan gods.
No Christian cross marks your permanent hotel. Just

four flags in cardinal directions, and later a headstone. I thought we were only visiting but now you are flying far away.

14.
You are flying far away and I am standing still.

Yesterday my father was dying

Yesterday my father was dying, and he asked me
why — in a voice so hoarse and dry I had to lean in close to
hear him — why I flew two-thousand miles. I asked myself:
about the odor from the cracked shell of his skin; about his
breath, which smelled as if he'd crawled from underneath
the house, or drifted up from ocean's depths, like the one
I flew across, only to borrow the truck he could not drive,
and race to a gas station for cigarettes, when I had not
smoked in years.

I sit out on his front porch swing, another thing
untouched since I've been here, and watch a trail of ants
raise a cricket from the ground. Paralyzed, swollen, and
I hope numbed, she drags her egg stick on the cement like
a broken magic wand, her feelers twitching uselessly as
they lift her up and carry her — like the clumsy paramedics
hauled my father to the funeral home.

We're all alone, I thought, that cricket and my
father's wife and me. And we can't grasp what carries us.
It isn't grief, at least not mine, that moves us to another's
house, for days or weeks, a time of strangers leaving
chicken made in casseroles, and frozen, labeled with dates,
names, and numbers, like toe tags, so we know where to
return the clean dishes and Tupperware.

I sit and smoke and stare in space, watch the insects
scale the bricks, not knowing if the cricket laid her eggs, or
where the ants will carry her, or if I give a damn what they
do with my father. How would I know what he wanted? I

wasn't here, and we weren't close. His wife should know better than to ask me if I care if she buries him in her hometown three states away; or if she keeps the urn; or if I want to share his ashes.

Though, maybe I do.

There is a hint of rain in this morning's humid air, and the ants have moved the cricket to the concrete's edge, where she teeters before falling in the weedy flower bed.

I find their nest. The sandhill's higher on the western side to keep the rain from rushing down and flooding them. The hole, too small to fit the carcass underground, is perfect for a final cigarette.

III.

The Best Way to Eat a Mango

My friend Hermes from Dominica says the best way
to eat a mango is "naked as the day you were born,"
and to prove it we take a chest full on crushed ice
across Pillsbury Sound. We walk from the ferry dock,
sharing the cooler's weight between us.

I have never seen Hermes naked; even now,
as we rest the chest and switch places, switch arms,
I take off my tank top but he keeps covered up.
Where the tight shirt doesn't cling to his arms
the sweat runs off his black skin like oil.
A bead falls from his brow

to his nose and he smiles at me. Solomon Beach
is nearly empty on Tuesday. We have hiked up a fever
and an appetite. The big Igloo barely dents the white dune
I run down, stripping to the sea,
leaving sneakers, shorts, briefs—a trail
like breadcrumbs any lover could follow.

I dive in quick and the shock is immediate.
Total refreshment like a dip in spearmint
or mentholatum, then Hermes beside me splashing.
Pushed into him by a wave, both of us laughing,
water washing innocent every brush
guided by buoyancy and current.

Face first on warm sand until its heat
expands my shrunken length; Hermes'
shadow as he stands in profile extends
like a sundial: time to turn over.
My Speedo tan line gets the joke,
the crisp contrast coated now like a donut.
"Cinnamon and sugar, mon," he says,

and pushes me with his toe. There is no
change in color to raw Dominican mahogany
and a bikini would be satirical: more banana than fig leaf,
if you know what I mean, a grown man
in boy's briefs. "Be free," he says
and asks if he can blindfold me.

"The juice will sting," he says. I protest.
If I close my eyes I'll miss the carnival
of flesh, yellow pulp and skin like ripe peaches.
"Taste test," he says, because there are fifty-two
types of mangoes and he's brought thirteen.

"There is no safe way to eat a mango in public,"
Hermes says, "but it is not a private fruit."
"When one sense is denied," Hermes says,
"the others compensate and become extrasensory."
When I become recognized as an islander,
Hermes says, the mosquitoes will quit biting.

The orange spot behind my blindfold fades
and then a sun a thousand times brighter

but ice cold rains across my face and I taste
the first: grafted mango. "Stay off de sun
or close to de water, mehson," Hermes imitates
his grandma. Thick juice drips down my skin.

"Bite." After thirteen I am sated and converted.
A total mess. Hermes leads me to the water
and unties my blindfold. "Wash off," he says,
"love sticky—attract bugs."

Sunday, Francis Bay

Jungle-living in a naked treehouse
my main character stands up and screams
"I'm finished!"   And what else but to listen
when he sings: a bush dove's purr

under our feet, the Eco-tent's
recycled plastic flooring squeak
our stringer of dented Diet Coke can chimes
the sea's wet repercussion

We were modest with wishes
but autumn's fortune won't be
silent, won't deny lungful explosions
remembering this high sun and season

Those planets lined up Friday
but now I'm out of whack
going to bed with pajamas on
an empty pad and pen beneath my pillow

(with fire)

Laura Palmer floated up all wrapped in secrets.
The diarist was torn from Hell between Bobby
Briggs and Snake, a strapless paperback
negligee in the grips of a boy
and an older man who thought Laura a thing to play,
a homecoming queen touched

by the devilish one. And Theresa Banks touched
a year before, Theresa Banks' secret,
plastic water-pruned nude, a bruised bitch played
like a restrained hand unrestrained, a girl robbed
of her filmy white dress, taken to Hell in back
of a truckstop at the end of the line by the boy

BOB shattered into erotic slivers, the boy
who as a man came to Laura's bedroom to touch
the hem of the monster he created, fighting back
the urge to pull the secret
over his own head, like the plastic bag BOB
gave Leland Palmer to play

with on his eighth birthday. BOB played
with the bag. BOB played with the boy.
The boy played with the bag and the boy played with BOB.
BOB taught the boy to touch
beneath the plastic, beneath the secret,
or else he-knew-what: BOB would come back.

And all these years later BOB had come back,
but this time he wanted to play
with Laura, Leland's secret
prize, the possession he suspected of affection for a boy
at school, or worse, a one-armed man touching
the tenderest part of the wound. It was BOB

who burned the cut-red scab, BOB
who took the tortured tattoo back,
removing limbs' liability, the ability to touch
the tongue of God, a taunt to play
with torment, to firewalk a boy
into secret manhood, a girl into a secret.

"Can you keep a secret, Bobby?"
Laura asked, her back to the boy
she played, the boy she touched

with fire.

Boca al Lupo

Red Ridinghood
broke blueberries
against the wolf's canines,
let their juice
purple her fingers.

To sweeten his nose,
Red Ridinghood chewed
cloves and ginger.

To sweeten his ears,
she sirened lullabies.

To sweeten his eyes,
she removed her cloak,
angled her head,
and let her maple hair
fall to reveal
her long Etruscan neck.

To sweeten his mouth
Red Ridinghood
bathed in oleander.

Full of Aloha

(a fiction)

Her name was Tiffani Hercules, but her married name is Limahai. In the neighborhood they call her Pity—Pitahaya, the Dragon Flower—a beauty unreliable to blossom. She started out with promise. She bloomed at hula; was a model student; class president at Kalaheo High. The teachers said she was full of aloha, and pushed her to test her grace and grind, but the combination of that kind of brain and beauty is hell to contain in a tall thin girl.

Next thing you know, she's in a high school fashion show, and then she's Miss Hawai`i, and jetting off to Shreveport, Louisiana, for Miss USA, where she scored a ninety-nine percent in the swimsuit competition, but didn't win. Back in '98, when they announced the top ten names, and didn't call out Tiffani, it was like the wool had been pulled from her eyes. She wasn't queen of anything—but fooling a bunch of local Kama`aina.

That's when her brain kicked in. And Tiff learned quick. She knew she had to ride that trick like a street paved with green lights—play "go, go, go" as sure as her eyes lit up her whole pretty face when she smiled, accepting her scholarship to Dominican College. That summer she lived fast on the fame of her last rich success, expanding her cotillion of luaus into parlor games of rush and throttle. Before she left for New York, she addressed the incoming freshman at Kalaheo High on pakalolo and ye`yo, sipping vodka tonic from her Nalgene water bottle. Tiffani told the class she was going away to become a doctor and would come home to Honolulu with a prescription for her people. She said they could expect to do it too, if they worked real hard—and kept to herself that it would take a miracle.

She thought she'd lied. She had no intention of ever coming back. But Tiffani was a small fish and New York an ocean of sharks and suckers. Her grades began to slip, and soon she was homesick for the big rough shore of north Hawai`i, her own people, and their faith in her.

She was deceived again. To prove she was still a titta, she had to marry a môk, and if she had to marry a môk, she wanted the loudest, ugliest king. She started looking for trouble. "Beauty is only skin deep," her mama warned her, but she knew that looks could get her far and high, and that every môk dreamed of having a queen by his side. She had the perfect smile, and John Limahai couldn't wait for her to bite onto his pistol.

She rode those first waves of crystal like Duke Kahanamoku, and John let out a whistle of smoke and said, "You'll never be rid of me, Hercules." She begged for his pipe, and he made her promise to wear her crown when she blew him. He went to the bathroom and brought out an old copy of *Penthouse* with Vanessa Williams on the cover and asked her, Was she willing to do this? Tiff lit up again. She said, "Hot damn. Feed me to the angels!"

There wasn't anything greener than her haole eyes craving more of this man and his icy methamphetamine,

which kept her thin after she had his baby. Her mama
took custody, while John took what was left of her and her
name. She weakened under the bump in their trunk and
lost her curves. But not her nerve. She and John started
dealing, and she started feeling like her old self again. She
had found the lucky combination: speed and money and
speed.

She'd have kept it going, too, if they weren't busted
three years into it, their names in all the papers because of
her fall from grace. She made her first court appearance
without a stitch of makeup on her face, wearing shackles, a
short skirt, and barefoot. But she smiled for the cameras.

The night before in prison, she had had a vision
of release. She saw herself rising like the Maiden of
Manoa, arced by the seven colors of sky. So Tiffani
began her resurrection from the ashes. She planned
her metamorphosis like she practiced her speech for the
judges. She copped a plea. She told them everything—
that she had to get clean and that she had to get a divorce.

It worked. Fifteen-thousand dollars bail, and then,
after turning state's evidence, and with mercy and a good
attorney, a deferred sentence and five years probation.
Now she's halfway through her rehabilitation and is the
new poster girl for island addicts. She's back on the talk
shows, giving interviews, and speaking to high school
students about the dangers of drugs, how it can happen to
anyone.

But she's not just anyone. She's got a book agent
holding an auction for her memoirs. They're talking ABC

Movie of the Week with Tiffani playing herself. How's that for a comeback? She's been acting like Tiffani Hercules all her life. She has the might and forbearance of the succulent Dragon Flower. And the next man who wants to take her for his wife will have to steal the fruit behind her fiery breath — just like the legend of the Pitahaya says. So go ahead and call her Pity. She is that cactus orchid cheating death.

Quiscalus quiscula

Quiscalus quiscula,
you small open country bird,
voice a rusty hinge,
you creak your vow
and drop your wings,
but lift your head
to tell me how you'll love me.

An unpracticed voice
earns an onomatopoetic name,
the Common Grackle,
but your recursive truth
reveals determination.

And when the sun glints
from your fine black feathers,
shoulders boasting
a prismatic cascade,
I call you songbird.

Summer Marriage

We urged the tide to disregard the moon
Part island from its shallow grassy lake
Anticipating echoes of the loons

A boundary waters honeymoon in June
The only sound my novice paddle's wake
We urged the tide to disregard the moon

But it did rise   and we raised our canoe
To portage our provisions lake to lake
Still anticipating echoes of the loons

Lost tent pole   fight   a quick monsoon
We bent to force a stake
Urging tide to disregard the moon

We crept inside the slanted afternoon
And slept another storm   a soaken break
Yet anticipating echoes of the loons

We woke with rain and ate and felt the swoon
Of making up   of wind across the lake
We urged the tide to disregard the moon
Anticipating echoes of the loons

The Museum of False Starts

Houses fear counting couplets
A burning down erasing

I would have if I didn't
Wanted to badly

Erased erases erase
The return address

Otherwise pretend
At full admission

Discount nothing
Return to this address

Not you to me
Vice versa false ends

No return to the museum
Of false starts

Arachnophilia

I must confess all sex intrigues me, exponentially, but
with sixteen furry legs involved, I'm glued to my window,
a voyeur without a web cam, watching jumping spiders
stalk and fight their hairy mates into submission. They've
bushy brows, two eyes (of eight apiece) enlarged for
hunting prey, and sometimes fate. They're *Salticids*, these
fascinating acrobats, and they're doing the spider nasty.
She is brightly moustached, as he is. They could both be
bearish sailors swabbing mops across a deck, dancing to
the tune of *Don't catch, Don't be caught*, and hoping for a
stolen glance that gives the notion *Catch, Be caught*. He
semaphores: "Are you interested?" She balks a leap, then
raises on her black hind legs and signals back, snow-white
front legs: "Read my abdomen." Iridescent invitation.
He dances for her. I get too close; my shadow on the
window pane sways her to shutters. So I have to go out to
the porch to catch their circle of combat poses, his jump,
her stuttered urge to flee, one hell of an embrace. She's
cunning, playing hard to get, darting in and out of slatted
shadows—where she'll offer him her home-spun wedding
bed, a silk hammock for guarding eggs, a cocoon of life-
long association. Or else, that's where she'll eat his head.

Still Life

sunrise shines a pink-peach
light on your blue silhouette
dressing curtains drawn open
your shoulder blades blink
behind a blond dust of lashes

Picasso's color palette demurs
to Degas dream spasms
flying bird creases
a leg of lamb—melon
striped with red and white prosciutto

cubed from a Prussian ballet dancer
the morning after romance
a moon eclipsed
catches the autumn sun cold

Chasing Pan

Goat god gather your shepherds
lustful satyrs   robust men
in skins of sacrificial animals.

Let them come to contest
body brawn in nightly ritual
to win the right by fight and feast

upon your horn of plenty.
Let the woodland worship
be unbridled for four days;

on the second host a hunt
of bestial frenzy   proud stags
who aim to draw and haunt

and ease your never-aging want.
Let the great rebels race
into the fray stampeding

competing to tame an unruly ram.
Lie with the beings
whose playing most pleases.

Release the gods and titans
to your reeded nights' commands.
Sleep beside them on the soft green land.

Let them spring erotic
into third day's dawn   celebrants
uncorralled by pastoral music.

A festival of hearty composition
and fruitful scores awarded
to the more inspiring fluters.

A grueling competition rising
under constellations   you are mounting
an Olympian decision.

Wilderness demon in the morning
they're leaving   returning renewed
to their flocks and their wives.

All save the one who is praying
you'll choose him   to stay
for amusement   abusement   for life.

Triolet

The city is so loud it burns
We turn to love and then unturn
When loving's painful mark we earn
The city is so loud it burns
A panic prior loving learned
We yearn for love and for love's yearn
The city is so loud it burns
We turn from love and then return

Pica pica

Bacchus' bird of practical magic
control your shiny heart

alone you are unlucky
eating insects for their charms

two bring merriment
weaving farmers   spinning damsels

winter and summer
oiled feathers and new

gazza with your quick caw caaw
you are law   Imperial Magpie

good news cousin to crows
kin by original animal

Let's do this again

We shared waking up; one of us had to be first
to open a sleepy eye, and spy on the other, proving
he was there, then to close it, denying thirst,
the urge to rise and pee, a day beginning after loving
lasted a whole night. Flesh found again
through wadded sheets — legs again, arms again.
Skin to skin again. Mouths again.
This could be routine if we don't panic,
follow urge to flee and ruin it,
take a different job and move away,
or find another lover somewhere along the way.
I'll keep this morning like a photograph—
you shaving at the sink, me watching from the bath.

The Gift of Flight

The magic of a witch's flight is not the broom.
It's in the faithful sweep of cleaning out the mind
of any room for disbelief. The witch can fly
because he takes the leap—and doesn't hold his breath.
He knows the gist of certain clauses in the laws
of sense and gravity and death. The catalyst
is in his chanted whispers: "*Horse and hattock,
horse and go.*" He feels the lift. It's not too high,
and so he finishes with, "*Horse and pellatis! Ho! Ho!*"
He rises from the sounds found in an ancient book.
But asked if magic words were what it took to fly,
his reply is "No! It takes fierce hair! Wicked shoes!"
which goes to show: The gift of flight is in one's attitude.

Books Available from Gival Press

Poetry

Adamah: Poème by Céline Zins; translation by Peter Schulman
    ISBN 13: 978-1-928589-46-4, $15.00
    This bilingual (French/English) collection by an eminent French poet/
    writer is adeptly translated in this premiere edition.

Bones Washed With Wine: Flint Shards from Sussex and Bliss
by Jeff Mann
    ISBN 13: 978-1-928589-14-3, $15.00
    Includes the 1999 Gival Press Poetry Award winning collection. Jeff
    Mann is "a poet to treasure both for the wealth of his language and the
    generosity of his spirit."
    — Edward Falco, author of *Acid*

Canciones para sola cuerda / Songs for a Single String
by Jesús Gardea; English translation by Robert L. Giron
    ISBN 13: 978-1-928589-09-9, $15.00
    Finalist for the 2003 Violet Crown Book Award—Literary Prose &
    Poetry. Love poems, with echoes of Neruda à la Mexicana, Gardea
    writes about the primeval quest for the perfect woman.

Dervish by Gerard Wozek
    ISBN 13: 978-1-928589-11-2, $15.00
    Winner of the 2000 Gival Press Poetry Award / Finalist for the 2002
    Violet Crown Book Award—Literary Prose & Poetry.
    "By jove, these poems shimmer."
    —Gerry Gomez Pearlberg, author of *Mr. Bluebird*

The Great Canopy by Paula Goldman
    ISBN 13: 1-928589-31-0, $15.00
    Winner of the 2004 Gival Press Poetry Award / 2006 Independent
    Publisher Book Award—Honorable Mention for Poetry
    "Under this canopy we experience the physicality of the body through
    Goldman's wonderfully muscular verse as well the analytics of a mind
    that tackles the meaning of Orpheus or the notion of desire."
    — Richard Jackson, author of *Half Lives*

Honey by Richard Carr
ISBN 13: 978-1-928589-45-7, $15.00
Winner of the Gival Press Poetry Award
"*Honey* is a tour de force. Comprised of 100 electrifying microsonnets .
. . The whole sequence creates a narrative that becomes, like the Hapax
Legomenon, a form that occurs only once in a literature."
—Barbara Louise Ungar, author of *The Origin of the Milky Way*

Let Orpheus Take Your Hand by George Klawitter
ISBN 13: 978-1-928589-16-7, $15.00
Winner of the 2001 Gival Press Poetry Award
A thought provoking work that mixes the spiritual with stealthy desire,
with Orpheus leading us out of the pit.

Metamorphosis of the Serpent God by Robert L. Giron
ISBN 13: 978-1-928589-07-5, $12.00
This collection "...embraces the past and the present, ethnic and sexual
identity, themes both mythical and personal."
—*The Midwest Book Review*

Museum of False Starts by Chip Livingston
ISBN 13: 978-1-928589-49-5, $15.00
Livingston - a "mixed blood" poet - presents a new approach to poetry
through his experience.
"...Chip Livingston makes the ordinary exotic, erotic and
extraordinary."—Ai

On the Altar of Greece by Donna J. Gelagotis Lee
ISBN 13: 978-1-92-8589-36-5, $15.00
Winner of the 2005 Gival Press Poetry Award / 2007 Eric Hoffer Book
Award: Notable for Art Category
"...*On the Altar of Greece* is like a good travel guide: it transforms reader
into visitor and nearly into resident. It takes the visitor to the authentic
places that few tourists find, places delightful yet still surprising, safe yet
unexpected...."
—by Simmons B. Buntin, editor of *Terrain.org* Blog

On the Tongue by Jeff Mann
ISBN 13: 978-1-928589-35-8, $15.00
"...These poems are ...nothing short of extraordinary."
—Trebor Healey, author of *Sweet Son of Pan*

The Nature Sonnets by Jill Williams
ISBN 13: 978-1-928589-10-5, $8.95
An innovative collection of sonnets that speaks to the cycle of nature and life, crafted with wit and clarity. "Refreshing and pleasing."
— Miles David Moore, author of *The Bears of Paris*

The Origin of the Milky Way by Barbara Louise Ungar
ISBN 13: 978-1-928589-39-6, $15.00
Winner of the 2006 Gival Press Poetry Award
"...a fearless, unflinching collection about birth and motherhood, the transformation of bodies. Ungar's poems are honestly brutal, candidly tender. Their primal immediacy and intense intimacy are realized through her dazzling sense of craft. Ungar delivers a wonderful, sensuous, visceral poetry." —Denise Duhamel

Poetic Voices Without Borders edited by Robert L. Giron
ISBN 13: 978-1-928589-30-3, $20.00
2006 Writer's Notes Magazine Book Award—Notable for Art / 2006 Independent Publisher Book Award—Honorable Mention for Anthology
An international anthology of poetry in English, French, and Spanish, including work by Grace Cavalieri, Jewell Gomez, Joy Harjo, Peter Klappert, Jaime Manrique, C.M. Mayo, E. Ethelbert Miller, Richard Peabody, Myra Sklarew and many others.

Poetic Voices Without Borders 2, edited by Robert L. Giron
ISBN 13: 978-1-928589-43-3, $20.00
Honorable Mention for Poetry—2009 San Francisco Book Festival.
Featuring poets Grace Cavalieri, Rita Dove, Dana Gioia, Joy Harjo, Peter Klappert, Philip Levine, Gloria Vando, and many other fine poets in English, French, and Spanish.

Prosody in England and Elsewhere:
A Comparative Approach by Leonardo Malcovati
ISBN 13: 978-1-928589-26-6, $20.00
The perfect tool for the poet but written for a non-specialist audience.

Protection by Gregg Shapiro
ISBN 13: 978-1-928589-41-9, $15.00
"Gregg Shapiro's stunning debut marks the arrival of a new master poet on the scene. His work blows me away."
—Greg Herren, author of *Mardi Gras Mambo*

Songs for the Spirit by Robert L. Giron
ISBN 13: 978-1-928589-0802, $16.95
A psalter for the reader who is not religious but who is spiritually inclined. "This is an extraordinary book."
—John Shelby Spong

Sweet to Burn by Beverly Burch
ISBN 13: 978-1-928589-23-5, $15.00
Winner of the 2004 Lambda Literary Award for Lesbian Poetry / Winner of the 2003 Gival Press Poetry Award — "Novelistic in scope, but packing the emotional intensity of lyric poetry..."
— Eloise Klein Healy, author of *Passing*

Tickets to a Closing Play by Janet I. Buck
ISBN 13: 978-1-928589-25-9, $15.00
Winner of the 2002 Gival Press Poetry Award
"...this rich and vibrant collection of poetry [is] not only serious and insightful, but a sheer delight to read."—Jane Butkin Roth, editor of *We Used to Be Wives: Divorce Unveiled Through Poetry*

Voyeur by Rich Murphy
ISBN 13: 978-1-928589-48-8, $15.00
Winner of the 2008 Gival Press Poetry Award
"*Voyeur* is a work of vision and virtuosity. Concerned with relationships, marriage, sex and power, the poetry is dense, rapid, dazzling, the voice commanding, the speaker charismatic...spectacular."—Richard Carr

Where a Poet Ought Not / Où c'qui faut pas by G. Tod Slone
(in English and French)
ISBN 13: 978-1-928589-42-6, $15.00
Poems inspired by French poets Léo Ferré and François Villon and the Québec poet Raymond Lévesque in what Slone characterizes as a need to speak up. "In other words, a poet should speak the truth as he sees it and fight his damnedest to overcome all the forces encouraging not to."

For a list of poetry published by Gival Press, please visit: *www.givalpress.com*.

Books available via BookMasters, Ingram, the Internet, and other outlets.

Or Write:
Gival Press, LLC
PO Box 3812
Arlington, VA 22203
703.351.0079